In Search of a Child

By

Christy Ogbeide

© 2002 by Christy Ogbeide. All rights reserved.

No part of this book may be reproduced, stored in a retrieval system, or transmitted by any means, electronic, mechanical, photocopying, recording, or otherwise, without written permission from the author.

ISBN: 1-4033-2465-4 (e-book)
ISBN: 1-4033-2466-2 (Paperback)

This book is printed on acid free paper.

1stBooks - rev. 10/10/02

Published by
El-shaddai Ministries
12111 Huntington Venture
Houston, Texas 77099

Dedication

To God the Father, Son and Holy Ghost.
To my darling, wonderful husband,
Dr. Emmanuel Omoruyi Ogbeide,
for his excellent support,
and to our miracle son,
Joshua Eghosasere Ogbeide.

Content

Dedication v

Acknowledgments ix

Foreword xi

A Poem xiii

Introduction xv

1. Early Childhood 1
2. Journey to America 7
3. Be Fruitful, and Multiply! 12
4. Deliverance from the Powers of Darkness 20
5. "Don't Give Up!" 34
6. Call to Ministry 41
7. "Vow and Thanksgiving" 54

Emmanuel's Story 63

8. Jesus The Anchor 66
9. God Knows My Telephone Number 77
10. Prayer and Fasting - "The Key to the Impossible" 95

Testimonies 104

Appreciation 106

Acknowledgments

I am truly indebted to several people,
who at various stages of my trial stood by me, through prayers,
love and concern.
My special thanks to my in-laws, family,
friends, and all Christian brethren.

Foreword

Two things about the Anointing

(i) It is tangible, and

(ii) it is transferable.

From my encounter with this book, I can testify that it is anointed, and directed of God. I pray that everyone who reads this book will encounter the tangible, transferable anointing this book carries in their lives and situations. Amen.

Tunji Osinulu

Dominion Sanctuary, Houston, TX

A Poem

"Joshua"

This home, patiently and painfully waited,
long, long years, for your arrival.
Welcome, miracle child; after hours begged,
days, weeks agreeing with months;
and years conniving to sluggishly crawl along.
Up there, you watched angels,
with our prayer power knocked down demons whom,
again and again delayed your homecoming.
Down here, gossip mongers galloped news
from mouths to ears; rumor peddlers faxed errands
from street to house.
Still, Papa believed the Word;
Mama to the Cross clung.
Welcome, faith baby, to a world in urgent need
of a <u>Joshua</u> generation.

by:

Dr. and Mrs. I. Agboaye (Godparents)

Introduction

In April of 1979, I got married to my wonderful husband Emmanuel Ogbeide, after which we relocated to the United States the following year. Then, we struggled to have children for fourteen years to no avail. It didn't matter that I was from a well-known Christian family, same as my husband but the waiting was long and painful. The inability to have children immediately after marriage can destroy the single most important expectation in a marriage.

Most women feel the loss of self-control and self-esteem to the point that someone like me became depressed and frustrated. In my case, I didn't feel like waking up in the morning. In my confused and depressed state I blamed myself, others and even God our creator for my problems.

My childlessness caused me a lot of despair and anxiety. Fear of being unable to bear a child in life, fear of being constantly ridiculed by many whom, innocently or knowingly did it. In fact, losing the dream of motherhood filled me with such grief that I consciously avoided places where there were children. This comes with lots of emotional stress and depression.

I pray to God any reader of this book will not go through what I went through, because of lack of faith in God; not knowing who I am in Him, and having been taken unaware by negative thoughts; forgetting that God is the God of impossibilities.

It may not be a child you are seeking for, it might be other needs like, life-partner, healing, prosperity, direction and so on; and it looks as if there is no way out; don't give up.

I pray sincerely for you, that you find strength in the word of God, His power and Grace, because He will surely take you through every storm and take you out of every valley of despair in Jesus Name. Amen.

"The Lord reigneth, Let the people tremble…" (Psalm 99:1). Life begins when God created Adam and Eve (Genesis 1:27). "And God created man in His own image, in the image of God created he him; male and female created he them." He commanded them to be fruitful and multiple and replenish the earth (Genesis 1:28). In fact, this is a commission God gave to man.

Sometimes, it is not always easy to accomplish, because of spiritual or natural causes. However, "we know that in all things God works for the good of those who love Him, who have been called according to His purpose" (Romans 8:28).

This book, "In Search of a Child" is written to encourage everyone, especially those whoput their trust in the Lord that there is hope and God's will must be done in our lives.

"For the Scripture saith, Whosoever believeth on Him shall not be disappointed" (Romans 10:11).

We must learn to put our trust in the Lord who never fails and never forsakes us, a God whose word is true and whose wisdom is deeper than anything that we can comprehend.

1
Early Childhood

I grew up in a typical Bini family in Benin City, Edo State, Nigeria, West Africa. A culture where the bearing of children is the prime thing in life or the person will be looked upon as a nobody. In fact, this happens in practically every culture in Africa.

The early part of my life was spent with my loving grandmother. I remember how my grandmother always made sure we went to school and concentrated on serving God. She always read her Bible for hours, although as an uneducated woman she did not understand what she was reading. But she could tell you every story in the Bible. She always talked about Jesus to make all that came around her know Him as their personal Savior.

I will never forget also, when I was growing up, my father always woke us up in the early morning hours for devotion. My dad was a banker and of the Anglican religion. He did all within his power to bring us up in a God fearing environment. We had to go to church, sing in the choir and tried as much as we could to be God-fearing children. As we were growing up, I discovered that the more I advanced in age, the more I wanted to draw closer to God, and the more I backslid when trials came my way.

I just had this belief that God our father had to take care of me, because it was His duty. So, I did not have to worry or struggle for anything. Through the help of my grandmother, and many others like my precious, kindhearted Aunt Mrs. Esther E. Smith, I always got whatever I wanted as a child. My grandmother's constant love, prayers and assurance, made me to grow up strong with a sense of security. Little, did I know that I would surely need this strong foundation the rest of my life. Remember, I said, I always got what I needed.

In 1971, I prayed that God should give me a husband that would love me even more than I loved him. Our faithful father answered that prayer, and allowed me to meet my husband that same year. At first, I had a very lukewarm attitude towards the relationship, because I did not believe that God could answer my prayers within two months. Anyway, God had His hands in our relationship. Three years after we met, he left for the United States to further his studies. We got married in 1979, and the following year, we were together in the United States.

The Battle To Get Pregnant

It has always been my desire to have children, so I thought it was that easy. I have always wondered when after some years couples get married and they don't have children; I concluded that probably they did not need any at the particular time.

After trying for a few months, we then decided to go and pay a visit to the doctor. I was 23 years old and wasn't used to seeing doctors except for minor things; so I was expecting to hear something simple like, "Stop worrying, all is well with you," I wasn't prepared at all to receive the kind of news that I heard. My own mother had seven children, so I did not see why I should have any problem having children.

After the doctor completed several different tests and examinations, he told me it appeared that I would have difficulty having a baby, if at all I will have any. The test results indicated that I have a big cyst on the left side of my ovaries. Nowadays, the common diagnosis is fibrous tissue, in my time it was cyst in the ovaries. He said, I had to take a lot of medication, if it does not work, surgery must then be done. This was not good news for me because all my life I had not undergone any surgery.

He said, most women suffering from ovarian cyst could only succeed in getting pregnant after doing the surgery.

During the following months my condition grew worse. The doctor gave me some more medication. My husband and I prayed and prayed and thanks be to God, miraculously in 1981, I got pregnant which was a very good sign that something good was happening in our life and that God has answered our prayers. Unfortunately, tragedy struck at the fifth month of the pregnancy and we lost the baby.

At this time of my life it seemed that every wall collapsed on us. The years that followed were painful and cloudy. The window of our life has been cracked. Something painful, something fiery has burst into our life and hurt us deeply.

And suddenly God was not so easy to see. The view that was so crisp had changed, I turned to see God, but His figure was distorted to me. God seemed to be at a distance at this moment. Although, I struggled to believe that tragedy and travesty were not on the agenda of the God we serve. James 1:17 says, "Every good and perfect gift comes from above..."

Refocusing On God

The Apostle Peter had to refocus on God during his time of trials and temptations. Drawing from his own experiences with pain, experiences we bury deep down in our heart of hearts, Peter dropped a bucket into his heart and poured the contents out on the pages of the New Testament letter that bears his name. In fact, Peter mentioned suffering some sixteen times and used eight different Greek words to make his point. His words and life were meant to encourage, strengthen and remind us of something we would prefer to forget.

"Beloved, do not be surprised at the fiery ordeal among you, which comes upon you for your testing, as though some strange things were happening to you" (1 Peter 4:12).

The fiery ordeal here quite expresses the "painful trial that burns in our lives." This pain we do not expect or welcome in our lives. I was choked on bitterness toward everyone, even God. However, Peter in his own experiences, makes us realize that our sufferings are not accidental - the heavenly father knows about it.

The pain is not even interfering with God's purposes for our lives. In fact, it is part of His purpose. According to David Walls, in his book, *Finding God In The Dark*, he wrote, "...when God our Maker and refiner turns up the heat, His desire is to reshape us, to mold us, to cause us to grow up spiritually. And all of us must daily face the process of maturing, but the maturing takes heat."

The fullness of joy comes when we have a deep sense of the presence of God in our lives. Joy occurs when our pain pushes us to depend upon our God, not ourselves. At this stage of pain, we have no other person to turn to but to rest upon His never failing arms. Deuteronomy 33:27, "The eternal God is thy refuge, and underneath are the everlasting arms; and he shall thrust out the enemy (the devil) from thee…"

The doctor did all they could to clean out the remaining part of the baby I miscarried on my birthday in 1982. I asked the doctor numerous questions why it happened; he looked straight into my eyes and said gently but clearly, "I am only a doctor, I am not God. It will be all right."

2
Journey to America

"God is our refuge and strength, a very present help in trouble. Therefore, I will not fear, though the earth be removed, and though the mountains be carried into the midst of the sea" (Psalm 46:1-2).

Coming to America was a great eye opener. The expectations and excitement were overwhelming. Our God who has the whole world in His hand made the journey like a piece of cake.

Entering the United States, with all the propaganda and good things I had heard, I was expecting to live a simple and rich life without any hassle. I immediately found out right from the airport that America is not a bed of roses. Like they say, "no free lunch in America." I became home sick. I had a great cultural shock. The society was far different from the one I was used to.

Adjusting was not easy and coping was painful. Starting life altogether as a newly wed couple in a foreign country was no fun. There were lots of adjustments to be made. I thank God for the backing and encouragement of my husband and many family members.

Although, we did not even know how to pray at this time, God was still very much with us. Everything went on fine. I got a job and started my degree program immediately.

I graduated after four years with a BBA in Business Administration with minor in Economics. I never failed to commit my marriage into the hands of the Almighty God; who is exceeding abundantly able to preserve all that we commit into His hands. My early marriage life was sweet and rosy; there was a lot of mutual understanding. However, our focus was to get good education while our prime goal was to have children. It never left our minds. It was causing us a lot of anxiety and stress. It became our prime focus and concern. We were praying and expecting but to no avail.

Our visits to the doctors became more frequent. Sometimes, twice a week. Seeking for help and looking for answers. We had behind our minds that *"heaven helps those who help themselves"* which is not scriptural. The phrase is of the devil. I thank God for doctors; they did all they could, but to no avail.

Problems Of Infertility

Couples with infertility problem always resort to technology and infertility doctors for help and the cost is overwhelming. The United States is known for their experts and professional doctors. According to Dr. Lye, a professor of Sociology at the University of Washington, couples without children are more likely to split up than couples with children.

It is also noted in a study that appeared in Psychology Today (1966), that when couples are trying to get pregnant, they get overly tense and anxious; and everything they do is planned around it. My diagnosis was always discouraging. There was no time I went to the doctor that I returned with any good news. I was scared, especially as I was at this time being referred from doctor to doctor. My case became something that no one could understand. I was becoming real weak in my faith and was praying less. I never understood what was going on in my life. I found myself in a bad situation, a Christian with a great burden to carry and no message to share.

A Call For Help

I always at this time remember the verse in Psalm 23, which says, "The Lord is my Shepherd, I shall not want." This 23rd Psalm right from when I was young has ministered a lot to me. I know fully well that there is power in the word and promises of God. Although, I was depressed and angry over my problems, I felt betrayed and hardly want to believe that there is anything that matters to me in life. I tried to meditate in my heart the words of God. I knew behind my mind that "with God all things are possible."

Everyday, the journey seemed far and long. I never knew when or how my dream would come through. *"In peace I both lie down and sleep, for thou alone, O Lord, only makest me to dwell in safety"* (Psalm 4:8). Through it all, like David, in Psalm 4, God is protecting us with His power, and I have the joy, security and peace that our heavenly father always offers for free. At this time, I finally realized that when we are in distress and all seems to be gone; we should never fail to know that God gives peace that can never be destroyed. He is the God of peace Himself. Blessed be His holy name forevermore. Amen. We have joy that can never be surpassed; the Bible calls it "joy unspeakable and full of glory." We have love that will never let us go: God's unconditional love. We have a sovereign Lord who can never lose control; He is the King of Kings Himself, who is always in control.

In the midst of all this, one day, I decided to write a letter to God. To tell Him all about what was going on in my life. I finally tore up the letter after I imagined that God had read it after showing it to him. God wants us to speak to Him through our Lord Jesus.

I then had a dream, I saw a big figure like a mountain, it was white, and I was at the bottom of this great big sculpture, and I said, "I know you are God, please heal my womb now." I woke up and was frightened, because I did not have any right to talk to God with such a commanding way. My pain was unrelenting, but I thank God for every moment that He had blessed me with. I pray that my life be used for His glory, that I might carry my burden with Christian dignity, and that out of my devastation and trials; may His kingdom become apparent to someone lost and in pain.

3
Be Fruitful, and Multiply!

"And God blessed them, and God said unto them, Be fruitful, and multiply, and replenish the earth, and subdue it:..." (Genesis. 1:28).

This is the command God gave to everyone, to reproduce. However, in several instances in the Holy Bible many women like me suffered barrenness. Rachel faced with the embarrassment of childlessness said, "Give me children or I die." (Genesis 30:1). Abraham and Sarah suffered because of lack of children. Like Zechariah and Elizabeth, they had been unable to have children, and like Zechariah and Elizabeth, they were now very old. Nevertheless, God promised a son to Abraham and Sarah, and she eventually gave birth to Isaac (Genesis 18:1-16; 21:1-7).

The birth of Isaac was a fulfillment of God's promise. It was a miracle, and it was a sign of God's care and grace for Abraham and Sarah. Other stories also surface in the Old Testament of which the most popular one was the story of Elkanah and Hannah. Hannah cried out in prayer to God for a

In Search of a Child

son, "the Lord remembered her," and she became pregnant and she had a son, she named him Samuel (1 Samuel 1:1-20). It is very obvious that reproduction is a part of that which God intended for all His creatures especially man.

Satan hates the gift of reproduction, which God has given to man. He hates it for several reasons. It is an act that he, Satan can not duplicate. He can only pervert, distort and attempt to corrupt it in a desire to rob God's people of their blessings and benefits. In addition, each time Satan is able to frustrate conception, he eliminates a potential worker for the Kingdom of God, who would have come to bruise its head. The Lord said, *"And I will put enmity between thee and the woman, and between thy seed and her seed; it shall bruise thy head"* (Genesis 3:15).

The specific goal of demons, in the area of reproduction, is to pervert the reproductive process, to cause perverse thoughts and sin to corrupt the reproductive act, and to prevent or frustrate normal healthy procreation. If Satan can prevent a child from being born that means one less potential believer with which he has to deal, in addition to the unforgettable torment and frustration caused for the couple in search of a child.

Although Satan is not able to completely frustrate the reproductive process, he attempts to surround it with as much of a corruptive taint, perversion, and impurity as he can. Sexual sins committed either before the act of marriage or after the act of marriage, tend to weaken the marriage union. Such sins cause doubts and fears, a lack of communication, a lack of intimacy, and otherwise impair the marriage relationship.

Sexual promiscuity of course, also opens the individual to the possibility of various venereal diseases, and sexually transmitted diseases, cruel abortions, selling of bodies for money; all these can serve as a self-inflicted judgment upon the sin, further frustrating and impairing the individual's ability to conceive. It is very necessary for both men and women to keep their bodies holy and pure until they are joined together in Holy matrimony.

God condemned fornication (that is having sexual relationship with someone to whom you are not married). Disobeying God's commandments (especially those concerning sexual relationships, involving relatives and other incestous relationships) can also make one eligible for the curse of childlessness.

> "And if a man shall lie with his uncle's wife, he hath uncovered his uncle's nakedness: they shall bear their sin; they shall die childless" (Leveticus 20:20).
>
> "And if a man shall take his brother's wife, it is an unclean thing: he hath uncovered his brother's nakedness; they shall be childless" (Leveticus 20:21).

However, for those who keep God's commandment and are faithful, God will surely sustain to the end. We can always count on Him to fulfill His promises. If He can oversee the forces of nature, surely he can see us through the trials we face. He has provided for all who turn to Him for strength. I know God has used my search for a child for fourteen years to open my eyes to the resources He has provided for all who turn to Him for strength.

I pray also that God will use your trials to show you your constant need of Him, and how He has sent His only begotten Son, Jesus Christ our Lord and Savior to deliver us from both the guilt and the power of sin. As, long as we thoroughly repent and forsake our sins.

Thus, we sometime see the mercy, grace and love of God towards even those who profess His name and try sincerely to live a God-honoring life in the midst of the most difficult circumstances. Searching for a child is one of the most devastating things, which no individual in this world will ever like to experience. However, for all God's people the issue of childlessness automatically become an issue of faith to be worked out in conversation with God.

"That the proof of your faith, being more precious than gold which is perishable, even though tested by fire, may be found to result in praise and glory and honor at the revelation of Jesus Christ" (1 Peter 1:7).

In this verse in the book of Peter, he talks about *"the proof of your faith"* or *the genuineness of your faith"* being proven by trials or tests. We should be constantly reminded that in both the New and Old Testaments for followers of God, like Abraham and Job, to mention but a few, it was through their trying circumstances that God checked whether their faith was genuine. This applies to all Christians.

In Search of a Child

The combination of faith and the creator reminds us of God's love and His power even in the midst of our pain. We should note that Christians do not suffer accidentally or because of irresistible forces of fate. We suffer according to God's will and plan. God is our creator and He's got the whole world in His hands; for that reason He is in control. He is faithful and sustains the world. We can always count on Him because God is faithful. We must always remember that His mercies endureth forever and are new every morning.

"Do you really want a child?", is a question I sometimes ask during counseling of women facing infertility. Some in their heart may not want a physical child due to their spiritual involvement, ancestral covenant and connection with "spirit husbands." God may decide not to bless a couple not properly join together also in holy matrimony. Also, many times the issues of infertility cannot be successfully resolved by the affected individuals until they have chosen to completely surrender their own wills to the will of God.

Personally, after searching and going through In-Vitro Fertilization (IVF) three (3) times which is also known as test-tube baby costing thousands of dollars; I turned to God. I changed my attitude towards Him by thanking Him for the blessings of the womb, instead of the previous attitude of murmuring and complaining. Your attitude can cause a delay or quicken God to solve your problem.

Having strong and unshakable faith, especially when everything else fails is a wise step to take. God honors faith and wants us to fully trust and depend on Him. One of my favorite songs is, *"Have faith in God, when your pathway is lonely, he sees and knows all the way you have trod..."*

Children are intended to be a blessing from God. *"Lo, children are a heritage of the Lord: and the fruit of the womb is His reward."* (Psalm 127:3) It is part of mankind in every culture. A person without a child is like someone lost in the world. In some places, such a person cannot even speak in the midst of his mates. "As arrows are in the hand of a mighty man; so are children of the youth. Happy is the man that hath his quiver full of them" (Psalm 127:4,5a).

Everyone would love to have their quiver full of children, including my husband and me. However, miscarriages, stillbirths, premature babies, low sperm count and the apparent inability to carry the baby to full term are still far too common in our age of sophisticated care and medical treatment.

Treatment for infertility is often extremely expensive, and it runs into thousands of dollars, (which we found out to our expense). However, seeking medical treatment can not be underrated, but with the full knowledge of when everything else fails, God cannot fail. Instead of giving up, we should fall into the ever-loving arms of our God, the miracle worker. He is the only one who excels in difficulties, and apparently loves to do the seemingly impossible. He turns very hopeless situations like mine into blessings. God is very able. I am speaking from experience.

However, not all infertility cases have a happy ending like mine. But please, do not give up. Stand on the promises of God. For, Sarah conceived and gave birth to Isaac when she was ninety years old. *"And Sarah said, God hath made me to laugh, so that all that hear will laugh with me"* (Genesis 21:3).

God will make all His faithful children laugh. It is a covenant between my God and me that anyone that hears or reads about my miracle son, Joshua; will surely have his or her prayers answered. I use my son as a point of contact to every such person seeking for God's miracle in Jesus Name. Amen.

4
Deliverance from the Powers of Darkness

"Who hath delivered us from the power of darkness, and hath translated us into the kingdom of His dear son: In whom we have redemption through his blood, even the forgiveness of sins" (Colossians 1:13-14).

As the years rolled by and there was no sign of my having a child, which I so desired, I decided to seek help where there was no help. I condescended so low as to worship other gods against God's first commandment.

"Thou shall have no other gods before me" (Exodus 20:3).

God warned us against serving other gods beside Him. God is a jealous God. I went through many rituals, drank herb medicines of different kinds, that I did not know where they came from, and the contents were unknown to me. Some really made me sick and to occasionally pass out.

My turning to traditional treatment (known as native medicine in Africa) made matters worse for me. The Holy Bible says in Psalm 115:3-8, *"The idols are silver and gold, the work of men's hand they have mouths, but they speak not: eyes have they but they see not: They have ears, but they hear not: noses have they but they smell not: they have hands, but they handle not: feet have they, but they walk not: neither speak them through their throat. They that make them are like unto them; so is everyone that trusteth in them."*

Through the worshipping of these idols, more demons came in and decided to torment and make my situation worse. Jesus himself made it clear to us that demons could cause a physical defect upon the human body. In Luke 13:16, as He ministered to the crippled woman; he said, *"Satan had her bound."* He cast the spirit of infirmity out of her and the same time our Lord Jesus "loosed" her from her infirmity making her whole again.

What Are Demons?

Demons are entities that no child of God should take for granted. Even Jesus Christ never took them for granted. He always cast them out. Demons are disembodied spirits. They long to have bodies through which to manifest their own lustful natures. Demon spirits work hand in hand to accomplish their goals. They are very good at what they do. Heaven knows that almost every case of physical problems has spiritual roots. The search to find the roots requires good detective work, fasting and praying, much patience, persevering, endurance, long-suffering, clear reasoning and spiritual discernment.

Frankly speaking, there are some cases of barrenness, which even the very best doctor, counselors and the couple themselves are unable to find any fault or anything wrong with them. But still, they are unable to get children. Many spiritual factors might be involved. Many different kinds of sins like unconfessed sin can give entrance to demon spirits into ones life that can cause blockage of blessings.

Bitterness

Bitterness truly complicates things for any one seeking for the blessing of the womb. Bitterness is a deep resentment and anger steaming from the feeling of having been cheated; seeing yourself denied what others possess or have easily acquired. This is one of the reasons when caring whole-heartedly for someone else's child can trigger the natural conception of another and break barrenness from the woman. The scriptures says, *"Looking diligently lest any man fail of the grace of God; lest any root of bitterness springing up trouble you, and thereby many be defiled..."* (Hebrews 12:15).

This scripture in the Bible really helped me to fight against bitterness especially for those who laughed and said hurtful words to me during my trials. Once you fall short of the grace of God, no matter the fasting and praying it will be to no avail. To get quick deliverance and healing especially when seeking for God's blessing of the fruit of the womb, the person has to let go of every form of bitterness, anger and malice towards anybody.

Fear:

> **"Fear not; for thou shalt not be ashamed: neither be thou confounded: for thou shalt not be put to shame" (Isaiah 54:4).**

Fear can quickly usher in doubts in one's life. For a woman seeking for a child, fear and doubt can further complicate, or even, cause the condition to get worse. Fear, of never going to have a child again especially as the biological clock is ticking. The calendar is a constant reminder that every year that passes is increasing the odds against the likelihood of conception. At a time, I threw away all the calendars in my home. This is because I kept looking, and more fear crept into my life. God is so good that age has nothing to do with when it is time for Him to perform His wonderful miracles in our lives.

Unforgiveness:

This can also open any person to the full influence of and infection with evil spirits by allowing unforgivness to take root. An unforgiving Spirit is very deadly to any person. Mark 11:25, *"And when ye stand praying forgive, if ye have ought against any that your Father also which is in heaven may forgive you your trespass."* The key to receiving your blessing quick is to forgive everyone that must have hurt you. Jesus Christ shed his precious blood for us all. He died for the sins He did not commit. So, there is actually no reason why any person cannot forgive anyone that hurts him/her. The grace and the Spirit of God can always help us when we think we can not forgive. Forgiveness is one the principles of the cross. Matthew 18 is an eye opener and therapy to forgiveness.

Love:

Roman 13:8 says, *"Owe no man anything but love."* 1 John 3:18, *"My little children let us not love in word, neither in tongue: but in deed and in truth."* We must love one another and live in peace with all men. Keep God's commandments, and it shall be well with you always. John 15:7 says, *"If ye abide in me, and my words abide in you, ye shall ask what ye will, and it shall be done unto you."*

Dreams:

God almighty reveals a lot to His children through dreams and revelations. As we lay down to sleep, we are unable automatically to control our sub-consciousness. Satan takes advantage of this very well. You wake up in the morning and have had a very bad dream, you have the authority in the blood of Jesus Christ to reject and rebuke every evil in that dream concerning you or your family members. Anything, that does not glorify God in your dream can be rejected and canceled in the mighty name of Jesus.

On the other hand, God very much reveals the future to us through dreams. I personally take dreams very seriously. I know very well that before any blessing manifests in the physical, be it in the area of healing, child-bearing and others, it must first be done in the spiritual realm. I had a dream about three weeks before I found out that I was pregnant; in that dream, a lady was pouring olive oil on my head saying in my dialect, "You will have a child, Okay."

Although, I was bleeding at this particular time, I held on to the dream, because I know Satan will not show me such a good dream. Just three weeks later, I found out I was pregnant. Glory be to God. In the old and new testaments, God appeared to several of His children in dream, instructing them and giving them orders on what to do.

During counseling, when I am confronted with cases that are seemingly impossible in human eyes, I always ask, "what revelation do you have about this situation?" Whatever one is going through, God will always speak. Genesis 28:10-11, *"And Jacob went out from Beersheba, and went toward Haran. And he lighted upon a certain place, and tarried there all night, because the sun was set' and he took of the stones of that place, and put them for his pillows, and lay down in that place to sleep. And he dreamed, and beholds a ladder set up on the earth, and the top of it reached to heaven: and behold the angels of God ascending and descending on it..."*

Dreams are very vital in human spiritual growth. Through dreams Satan and his cohorts can cause sickness, barrenness, place curses and so on. But it can be broken and reversed with the precious blood of Jesus Christ our blessed savior. My prayer always is committing of my dreams, consciousness and subconsciousness into the hands of God and also covering my body, soul and spirit with the blood of Jesus. When Satan the enemy sees the blood, he shall pass over.

Curses:

In many countries which still practice superstitious forms of pagan religion, especially those which employ witchcraft, it is common to hear of curses being spoken to cause childlessness, barrenness, or death for all future children. It is very frightening for a woman to be told that a curse has been placed on her preventing her from childbearing. The good news however, especially for those of us from Africa, is that God is greater than all the power of the entire witches and wizards and all their spells, charms or curses. Our God is God of all! Jesus, who loved the little children, still loves little children and those who would be their mothers. God has made provision to break all the power of the curses aimed against motherhood and all His children.

Bondage:

According to the dictionary "Bondage" means a state of subjection to a force, power, or influence. Satan can subject you to compromise and turn you from your faith, unless you know who you are in the Lord.

During my search for a child, I was told to abstain from some of my favorite foods like okra soup. Ostensibly, they were the cause of my problem. Somebody I know was asked to throw away all her red and favorite clothes. I was made to recite certain incantations standing in a certain position at a particular time of the day and counting what I recite. It was all bondage. I was made to perform sacrifice and throw lots of food into the river. Unless you know who you are in the Lord, you can be deceived and fooled by the devil. The messengers of Satan, like their master have wealth of experience in deceiving people.

How Do We Revoke Or Break Curses?

Curses inherited as a result of sins by our predecessors can be reversed. *"Christ hath redeemed us from the curse of the law, being made a curse for us: for it is written, Cursed is everyone that hangeth on a tree" (Gal*atians 3:13). Our Lord Jesus Christ has paid the price. He came to SET THE CAPTIVES FREE. He came so we might have life and life in abundance. I thank God for Jesus and for a scripture like *"For this purpose the Son of God was manifested that he might destroy the works of the devil.* (1 John 3:8)

We can break curses by sincerely reading and understanding the word of God; and with the blood of Jesus Christ. Believe in the words and the power in the word. Have solid faith in God. Reaffirm your faith in Jesus and His completed work on the cross of Calvary. In the presence of a witness, verbally and prayerfully renounce and break all ties with ancestral spirits, spirit husbands, ancestral and inherited covenants with the blood of Jesus, and thank God for what He has done. Once curses are broken, the legal grounds used by demon spirits to remain in a person's life are taken away. Hallelujah!

Let Us Pray:

I (your name), a redeemed child of God by the blood of Jesus Christ, today renounce and break all covenants with any spirit husband and children and all ancestral spirits - whether made by me or on my behalf. Such covenants whether made knowingly or unknowingly, in the physical or in the spiritual. Today Lord, I declare freedom from all their influences and enslavement. As Jesus is alive from the dead, the goodness and fruitfulness of the kingdom of God almighty shall ever be my inheritance UNDISTURBED in Jesus Victorious name I pray. Amen.

I (your name) close all door where the enemy (the devil and his demons) have gained entry into my life. I ask you my Lord in Heaven to seal these areas with the precious blood of Jesus Christ. Amen.

In fact, the above prayer really was a blessing to me during my trial. When God seals all entrances of Satan and its cohorts to your life your blessing must surely and truly manifest in Jesus Name. Amen.

Hindrances To Receiving Deliverance

There are however hindrances that can hamper our deliverance. People run from one preacher to another seeking deliverance. First of all only God can deliver you. A preacher can pray for deliverance but the preacher does not have control over your life style that might open doors for the demons to come back. It is hard to cast out demons when you have their property.

It is hard to send them away when you have things that invite them back and open doors for them. The following are some doors to demons; curses, sin, pride, passiveness, ungodly soul ties, occultism (magic power), fear (the opposite of faith), embarrassment, unbelief (demons of unbelief are wicked, they make you think even salvation is fake), lack of desire to be saved (some want the healing but not the healer).

Unforgivness:

This is one of the greatest door opener to demons. Mark 11:25 says, *"if you do not forgive neither will your heavenly father forgive you."*

Lack of knowledge is no excuse. The Bible says that the people perish because of lack of knowledge. Bitterness as previously mentioned; living an unholy life, to mention buta few can hinder prayers. Maybe, you do not understand the gravity of the sins you are committing, always ask God to show you the cause of your problem. He is kind enough to let you know about your sins through the conversion of the Holy Spirit, so you can adjust and repent.

Many churches do not even want to talk about demons and how they operate. Satan loves it when he is not being exposed. We have to expose him and bind him in Jesus name. Repentance brings about quick deliverance. The Bible says except we repent *"we shall all likewise perish"* (Luke 13:5). Repentance and forsaking of sins is you turning around and turning away from sin. It is the result of godly sorrow. "Godly sorrow worketh repentance to salvation" (2 Corinthians 7:10). After thorough repentance comes the actual breaking of the curses. And this is done in the name of Jesus. We have the authority to break curses based on Galatians 3:13.

How To Stay Delivered

It is necessary after having been delivered by the power of God Almighty through His son Jesus Christ, to keep your deliverance. If the person is not careful, the spirit might come back and inhabit its place and the state of the person may become worse. (Matthew 12:43-45)

Ways to keep your deliverance are:

Read Your Bible Daily: Pray frequently in your understanding and also in tongues if you already have the prayer language; and always plead the blood of Jesus on yourself and your family. The mind is the battlefield, so you must cast down evil imaginations, and bring every thought to the obedience of Christ Jesus. (2 Corinthians 10:5)

Pray To The Father Fervently: Pray without ceasing (Luke 18:1), more than three times a day, asking Him to make you alert, sober and vigilant against wrong thoughts and doings. (1 Peter 5:8,9)

Make Sure You Are Alert: Be alert about any signal the demons want to introduce by reminding you of your past and trying to come back. Speak boldly, and openly reject and denounce his thoughts and advice.

Make sure you are not partakers of the Lord's table, and of the table of the devil (1 Corinthians 10:21) Lastly, know how to use your authority against demons. Stand against him with the blood of Jesus. Try as much as possible to stay clean and keep God's commandments by asking God to direct your paths and ways. Proverbs 3:6 says, *"In all thy ways acknowledge Him, and He shall direct thy paths."*

Bind the demons and loose upon them the spirits of destruction (1 Chronicles 21:12), burning and judgment (Isaiah 4:4), from the Lord Jesus Christ. Also, loose warrior angels upon the demons and ask the angels of the Lord to do battle for you in Jesus name. (Hebrews 1:14; Matthew 18:18)

Remember that the Lord said that whatsoever we bind on earth is bound in heaven and whatsoever we loose on earth is loosed in heaven.

I pray God in the name of Jesus Christ to deliver you from all oppressing, possessing, ancestral spirits, in Jesus Name. Amen. When the spirit of barrenness has been broken, blessings automatically manifest in the physical.

5
"Don't Give Up!"

"Why art thou cast down, O my soul? And why art thou disquieted within me? Hope in God: for I shall yet praise him, who is the health of my countenance, and my God" (Psalm 43:5).

When faced with a situation and there seems to be no way out, look up to Jesus and don't give up. Have faith and believe and call upon the Lord with clear conscience and keep His commandments. Giving up means giving the devil and his demonic servants cause to rejoice. Many times in my life during the ordeal, I truly wanted to give up. I felt then that it was better for me not to have been born at all than go through the big shame and humility of not having a child.

I became the reproach of many. I always felt that the earth should open up to swallow me. It was normal of me to feel that way. But that did not solve the problem. In fact, the more depressed I was, the worse my problem. Sometimes, dear readers, God himself allow these trials to happen, as a proof of our faith and to draw us closer to Him. For the past years, I have

In Search of a Child

been ministering; I thank God because the trials I went through, have helped to strengthen my faith and caused me to have patience in dealing with other fellow human beings.

<u>Sometimes God allows it to Happen</u>

> **"Now there was a day when the sons of God came to present themselves before the Lord, and Satan came also among them. And the Lord said unto Satan, Whence comest thou? Then Satan answered the Lord, and said, From going to and fro in the earth, and from walking up and down in it." v. 12, "And the Lord said unto Satan, Behold, all that he hath is in thy power; only upon himself put not forth thine hand. So Satan went forth from the presence of the Lord" (Job 1:6-7;12).**

From the above Bible reading, it is obvious that God Himself was giving Satan permission to try Job's faithfulness to Him. We know the rest of the story, that even when Job lost everything, he still remained faithful and devoted to God. Job is a typical example. Another case of God's trying His children was with Abraham when God told him to go and sacrifice Isaac,

Christy Ogbeide

his son of promise. Many of us like me at this instance would probably have mistaken God's voice for that of the devil. But praise God for faithful people like Abraham, he obeyed God and as you know the story God provided a lamb for the sacrifice. For every test passed, there is spiritual and physical promotion. Everything we go through, God knows about.

Another case in point was Daniel, who never gave up on God, when due to his faith and belief, he was thrown into the lion's den. God sent angels to shut up the mouths of the lion and he came out unhurt. Oh, what a wonderful God we serve. Like the song goes, *"if there is no trial, how can we know what the Lord can do…"*

Trial: Living By Faith

"But we have this treasure in earthen vessels, that the excellency of the power may be of God, and not of us. We are troubled on every side, yet not distressed; we are perplexed, but not in despair; Persecuted, but not forsaken; cast down, but not destroyed; Always bearing about in the body the dying of the Lord Jesus, that the life also of Jesus might be made manifest in our body" (2 Corinthians 4:7-11).

Although we are troubled on every side, but as children of God we cannot be distressed. We are faced with trials but cannot be despaired. I heard of a pastor who lost all five children in one day. They were all in the car when the parents left the car with the engine on to do a quick stop to see somebody. One of them just went on the steering wheel and drove the car into river and all drowned. Thank God the couple is still preaching the gospel till today. God only knows why and what happened. God is faithful always. It is true that Christians face a lot of trials. But the Lord said in Psalm 34:19,

"Many are the afflictions of the righteous: but the Lord delivereth him out of them all" (Psalm 34:19).

Actually, in times of trials we need God's wisdom to deal with it. Often, the pain is so severe; the trauma so unsettling, that we have difficulty accepting them let alone understanding them. However, a faithful Christian sees life and its everyday problems from God's perspective, and as a result, is able to see those problems as opportunities for growth.

We must at this point, instead of giving up, choose to obey God's voice, read our Bible daily and stand firmly on God's promises and words. Our Lord Jesus told us that in this world we will have tribulations, but we should be of good cheer because he has overcome the world. (John 16:33)

Peter and Andrew, had problems, they had bags of experience in fishing, but on this particular day, there was a problem, they had toiled all night but caught nothing. Jesus at this particular time came by, unknown to them that he is the Lord and the Messiah; he simply commanded them to throw their net into the sea in the morning, contrary to the principles of fishing. They never knew him before but they did obey Jesus. The Bible says, "And Simon answering said unto him, Master, we have toiled all the night, and have taken nothing: nevertheless at thy word I will let down the net" (Luke 5:5).

Victory Through Our Lord Jesus

"There is victory in Jesus, our savior forever" as the song goes. The Bible says, *"But thanks be to God, who giveth us the victory through our Lord Jesus Christ" (1 Corinthians 15:57).*

Jesus gave us victory through his death on the cross. Jesus has given us victory and so we shall lift up His name forever. Giving up is a waste of time because God is working out everything according to His purpose. The thoughts God has for us are not of evil but of good (Jeremiah 29:11). Our trying experiences today are preparing us for a glorious tomorrow. When Christ returns and we see Him, we will bring "praise and glory and honor" to Him if we have been faithful in the sufferings of this life.

Apostle Peter reminds us that God's purpose in our present grief may not be fully understood in a week, in a year, or even in a lifetime. In fact, some of God's purposes will not be known until when believers die and go to be with the Lord. But He promises great reward to all those who put their trust in Him and endure to the end. As Christians our response to trial is not to give up but to believe.

Believe - means *"to trust or rest our confidence in someone, to depend on them"* It is the ideal of resting totally all your being in Christ. It is one thing to believe and another to trust. Personally, I never at the early stage knew how to trust fully. I believed God was too slow about solving our problems. But the answer to all our problems as children of God is taken from Roman 8:28-32, *"And we know that all things work together for good to them that love God, to them who are the called according to his purpose."* v. 32, *"he that spared not his own*

Son, but delivered him up for us all, how shall he not with him also freely give us all things?"

Frankly speaking, as I fully trusted in the Jesus Christ, fullness of joy came into my life. I felt a deep sense of the presence of God in my life. Jesus made it clear, as does Peter, that joy is inseparably connected to love and trust, and that there can be joy in suffering when it is seen to have a redemptive purpose.

We should always remember that "no trial, no victory." Don't give up - hold on to all the promises of God, which are "Yea and Amen" in Christ Jesus (2 Corinthians 1:20). Always remind the Lord of his promises and He will surely bring to pass the fulfillment, at his own appointed time.

God is never too late. His time is the very best. *"For the vision is yet for an appointed time, but at the end it shall speak, and not lie: though it tarry, wait for it; because it will surely come, it will not tarry" (Habakkuk 2:3).*

Don't give up, it shall come to pass. It will be well.

6
Call to Ministry

"Also, I heard the voice of the Lord, saying, Whom shall I send, and who will go for us? Then said I, HERE AM I: SEND ME" (Isaiah 6:8).

The Bible says that, *"for the gifts and calling of God are without repentance" (Roman 11:29).* The good Lord has commissioned everyone in a special way to go into the world and preach the gospel (Matthew 28:19). But little did I know that it would come strongly on me during the darkest moment of my life. At this particular time, my case was completely hopeless, so much that I went to two new doctors on separate occasions. Each one of them wrote on my case note after seeing me "no charge" and refused to call me back.

In fact, my case was a hopeless case. The scar tissues around my ovaries and fallopian tubes, caused by the numerous surgeries, made it impossible to get pregnant. The scar tissues in fact covered the tubes and there was practically no hope of any kind. This is because there is no known medication that can take away scar tissues, except surgery, as one doctor told me.

Unfortunately, after giving him thousands of dollars for the surgery, another doctor then told me that the surgery created even more scar tissues and made the matter worse. Oh! I hated going to the doctor then because they truly had nothing but bad news for me. Unbalance hormones that are vital to pregnancy complicated the matter of scar tissues.

All hope was truly gone. Unhappiness was not uncommon with me. I was like the Lord Jesus who as the prophet Isaiah prophesied, was a man of sorrows and aquainted with grief" (Isaiah 53:3).

It was in the midst of this great storm, that the good Lord decided to call me to serve him.

At this time my whole life to me had come to an end. No hope of any kind. But the good news is that where we end is where God begins in our lives. For the simple reason that His ways are not our ways, neither are His thoughts our thoughts. Isaiah 55:8-9, *"For my thought are not your thoughts, neither are your ways my ways, saith the Lord. For as the heavens are higher than the earth, so are my ways higher than your ways, and my thoughts than your thoughts."*

Every calling of God is a high calling. Every placement is a high placement with the ultimate end to glorify Himself in the life of the person He has called.

Of course, we are not just created to wake up in the morning, eat, drink and go to work. Instead our Maker and Creator has a designed purpose for everyone he created. He knew us even right from our mother's womb. He set some of His special children apart in order to glorify Himself. I thank God that I am one of them. *"For whom He did foreknow, he also did predestinate to be conformed to the image of his son that he might be the firstborn among brethren"* (Romans 8:29).

It was beyond my own human understanding that at this lowest moment of my life God called me to "set the captives free."

> **"The Spirit of the Lord is upon me, because he hath anointed me to preach the gospel to the poor; he hath sent me to heal the brokenhearted, to preach deliverance to the captives, and recovering of sight to the blind, to set at liberty them that are bruised" (Luke 4:18).**

God is good; He starts from where you think you have ended. At first, I refused to work for God or obey His calling. This is because it would expose me to more ridicule. I pleaded with the Lord to please bless me first with a baby before going into the ministry, so that I would have a testimony to show. After days of asking Him to bless me first before going into the ministry, our Lord promised me that he would bless me and bless His children if I obey His voice.

On October 23, 1991, in my dream the Lord said, "Why don't you start the Jesus Women fellowship, on October 26 in Houston, Texas." The date to begin was told to me in the dream. However, the Bible says, to obey is better than sacrifice (1 Samuel 15:22b).

A woman that has no child getting into the ministry in a foreign land was no fun. But the good Lord was with me. I then began to bear other people's burden. *"Bear one another's burdens, and so fulfill the law of Christ" (Galatians 6:5).* My attention now switched from thinking about my childlessness every moment to concentrating on the Ministry.

Step by step my Lord was carrying me on, and the ministry began to grow. The sisters attending the fellowship amazingly now took my problem as a task that must be done. They prayed heaven down on my behalf. Dear readers, don't be deceived, where everything else fails, corporate prayers work fast. As I was praying for them they were praying for me.

Few days before the ministry started, my husband woke up, pulled me from the bed, we both found ourselves in kneeling position, he said, "Oh my wife, go and do God's work please."

I asked him why, because apparently, he was not very much in support few days ago when I told him about what the good Lord was communicating to me about ministering to women. He then, said, "Jesus came into this house last night and walking through that corridor. He said to me, 'I want to use your wife.'" Since then my husband has tremendously supported the ministry and my calling.

Dreams:

God always speaks to His children through dreams. In my dream, people would be praying for me or I would see myself taking Bible examinations. I honor God for my calling. A friend of mine in 1989 called me up in the early morning hours and narrated her dream to me. That she "saw me in her dream in a room praying loud with lots of women." I discarded the dream because I did not see how I could be praying for women or people when I had no child.

Calling:

Every calling has its terms and benefits of service. A Ministry is an appointment you do not apply for and cannot retire from. Every calling of God like my own is an appointment by Him. A call to Minister enlists you automatically in the forefront of God's army with Jesus as the Captain. There is great reward and the best job with the great insurance on you and family combined with wonderful security. It was truly clear to me as the ministry proceeded that it was no child's play. God wants us to take His work serious in any area and capacity we are called to service.

Actually, when God calls you for a special assignment it is not the same as just going to Bible school to get a degree. Make sure you have an appointment call and assurance before going into the ministry.

It is not a quick money-making place or somewhere to get popularity and get rich quickly. In fact, genuine preachers that deliver undiluted messages without compromising are the most unpopular in the society. As Jesus said, the world does not like the truth. Fortunately, it is only the truth that can set us free.

There are very many ups and downs in the ministry so much that if one is without special anointing one may want to quit. No person that puts his hand on the plough and looks back is fit for the kingdom of God.

The early days of the ministry were really tough and rough. On one occasion, Satan wanted to play his ugly trick on me. It was a Saturday, before I found out that I was pregnant, we did not find a place to fellowship. I was strongly discouraged.

When we got to the house we were to use for the meeting, the people were not at home. Thank God for the sister who was with me. She said we should hold the fellowship inside the car. "In the car?!", I exclaimed. "People might think we are crazy." "It is better that they think we are crazy, than not to hold the fellowship and disobey God", was her response.

She did truly encourage me. We then parked in front of the house, sang songs of praise (like a normal fellowship), prayed and went home. God is very faithful.

The very next day, which was on a Sunday, I saw a pastor who offered us a place to fellowship, without asking him. Just a few days later, I discovered that I was pregnant. Thank God in heaven that gave me the enablement to be faithful to Him.

At this period of my life, I was very shy and afraid to talk in public, and scared of large crowds. I could hardly maintain eye contact for more than two minutes. Why the Lord chose me among other persons for this particular assignment in His kingdom, still remains a mystery to me.

However, like God told Moses, *"He made the deaf and the dumb."* He called me to glorify Himself. Glory be to God. He then automatically released His grace at the same time upon me to enable me perform the task, Afterall, *"God himself has promised that he will never leave us nor forsake us"* (Hebrews 13:5b). God is also calling you today to serve him in Spirit and in truth. Obey His call and you will never remain the same.

Anointing:

After the call, God sends His special anointing upon the one He has called so that he/she will be able to administer and accomplish the assignment. Anointing is not a feeling; it is a sign of sanctification for consecration. No servant of God can get anything done without God's anointing. It is the anointing that makes things work and break every yoke on the way. The anointing transforms. It makes you become another person. I was truly transformed, boldness replaced shyness. *"And the Spirit of the Lord will come upon thee, and thou shalt prophesy with them, and shall be turned into another man"* (1 Samuel 10:6).

In Search of a Child

The anointing of course is the promise of the Father to everyone. The anointing protects and guides. The Bibles says, "touch not my anointed and do my prophet no harm." In my dream way back in 1986, I saw the following words written out on the wall, "For Ye Are My Anointed." Not understanding what it meant then, I called a pastor family-friend who explained what the dream meant.

Obedience:

I want to encourage all readers that no matter the circumstance, please always obey the voice of the Lord. Disobedience brings curse and not blessing. (Deuteronomy 28). Without obeying God, I may probably have remained barren till today. In fact, this was the hardest part of the trial, starting a ministry with no knowledge and with a problem that to us all looked impossible. No matter the amount of fasting and praying you are doing, without sincerely obeying the command of God by doing what He has asked of you, there cannot be a breakthrough.

In some instances, our merciful God, will force you like Jonah in the Bible who ended up in the belly of a fish; before he knew that God was really serious about him going to Nineveh which he had previously refused to go. I heard of a story of a brother whom God sent to Africa but refused to go because the mother-in-law, wife and daughter will not find it convenient.

However, Psalm 115:3, Says that *"God almighty does whatever pleases Him."* So within a year, the brother was reported to have, in two separate occasions, lost the mother-in-law and the wife. The Lord according to the story asked him, "now they are gone, who will delay you now? I pray that we should always hear the voice of God and do His will in Jesus Name. Amen. It is costly and can really be dangerous and can result in a bad and painful experience. Nothing should stand in our way in obeying God's voice.

Benefits:

Without doubt everyone knows that there is great reward in obeying the Lord without reservation. *"He that reapeth, receiveth wages" (*John 4:38). *"Even so hath the Lord ordained that they which preach the gospel should live by the gospel"* (1 Corinthians 9:14). *"The Laborer is worth of his hire"* (Luke 10:7).

When Abraham received his call to move from his country where he was so close to all his family, he sincerely obeyed. And the result was that God made him father of nations. God's paycheck is very big when we obey. It might not be a call to the ministry but like Abraham, it might be moving from your present location to help others.

I know of a preacher who said, he had forty-eight suits in his closet. He loved all of them and adored them, until one day, God told him to give all the suits away except one. Some of us will sincerely disobey. It is not very easy to do especially when you think of the money you have invested in them and also the fulfillment of having the suits. Anyway, all those suits went away in a minute when the call to give them out came.

Thank God he did, he is one of the most anointed preacher I have ever seen. It might be a call to forgive someone that has terribly hurt you or God waking you up at 3:00 am to pray for someone. Believing God for who He is during this time of change brings peace to one's life. Only God knows what is delaying blessings. Obey his voice and the miracle will be your portion.

Miracle:

Exactly seven months after the ministry started, God fulfilled His promise to me. I never knew I was pregnant because I was too involved in the things of the Lord. Against all odds, I was even bleeding but I kept on thanking God for the bleeding and every situation because God knows the best. Since I have obeyed Him to do His will, I was very confident that though the blessing tarries, it shall surely come to pass. I also know that delay does not mean denial. He will surely bless you. Just trust and obey for there is no other way. Do whatever God is asking you to do. God Almighty will not let you down. He will surely minister to your needs.

I thank God that I am a living testimony. I was so happy when I was told that I was pregnant, that I even requested the nurse that did the pregnancy test to give me a written confirmation letter, which she did. Glory be to God, I shouted for joy praising God all over the clinic. The mystery of fourteen years of childlessness was unfolding before my eyes in a second.

Whose Report Will You Believe?

We must believe the report of the Lord. His report says we are blessed and we shall be fruitful and multiply. His report says, Luke 1:37, *"For with God nothing shall be impossible."*

After I Got Pregnant:

Proverbs 10:22 became my medicine that I took every day. It says that, *"The blessing of the Lord, it maketh rich, and He added no sorrow with it."* After the blessing has come, do not let the devil steal it by bringing fear of what has happened in the past to your mind. Cancel immediately every negative thoughts and bad dreams and focus on Jesus. Even those around will like to say, "I hope this will not end up like before." Say "No!" because it is not your portion. Do not compromise at all with the devil and his ugly thoughts. Stand on the word of God constantly, stay away from anger and uncleanness so that the devil will not contest your blessing.

Oh, praise God. My son Joshua was born without any complications. This is truly a miracle my doctor said. God is a God of miracles indeed. Don't give up, unless you see what God cannot do. Of course, there is nothing that our God Almighty can not do. Like a family friend who came to see us after Joshua was born said, *"I am happy, this happened in my life time."* Praise God!

7
"Vow and Thanksgiving"

Vows are earnest promises or pledges that binds one to perform a specific act or behave in a certain manner.

"Offer unto God thanksgiving; and pay thy vows unto the Most High; and call upon me in the day of trouble: I will deliver thee, and thou shalt glorify me" (Psalm 50:14-15).

As explained above during the time of serious crisis and pain there is tendency to make a series of vows, but often times, as soon as the blessings come many forget to pay their vows unto the Lord and some people make vows they can not fulfill. It is very dangerous. Making of vows brings quick attention to ones need. No one can bribe God, it is because of His mercies and grace that He even gives us all that we have.

Nevertheless, in the Old Testament, Hannah out of desperation made a vow. *"And she was in bitterness of soul, and prayed unto the Lord, and wept sore. And she vowed a vow, and said, O lord of hosts, if thou wilt indeed look on the affliction of thine handmaid, and remember me, and not forget thine handmaid, but wilt give unto thine handmaid a man child, then I will give him unto the Lord all the days of his life, and there shall no razor come upon his head" (1 Samuel 10-11).* God in His faithfulness heard the cry of Hannah and blessed her.

Another, instance of vow making is taken from Genesis 28:20 which says,

"And Jacob vowed a vow, saying, If God will be with me, and will keep me in this way that I go, and will give me bread to eat, and raiment to put on, so that I will come again to my father's house in peace; then shall the Lord be my God: and this stone, which I have set for a pillar, shall be God's house: and of all that thou shalt give me I will surely give the TENTH unto thee."

A vow is a vow. It comes from the heart and touches the heart of God. During my trials, on three different occasions I made vows. One instance was when we went on a vacation to Florida. Before we left, I had an urge to pray with someone on the prayer line and make a vow. In fact, that was my first time, I can remember making a vow. We then went on to vacation. The second day on the parking lot of Disney World, a big van collided with our car and itwas completely destroyed. I passed out for several minutes.

By the time they revived me and got me out of our brand new car, I knelt down on the parking lot and made another vow to serve the Lord all the days of my life. Looking back at the accident nobody could believe that my husband and I came out alive because even all the glass and tires were scattered. The third instance was when I was very sick in the hospital, in August 1989. In fact, till today it is amazing that I am alive. In four days I lost ten pounds in weight; I was unable to talk or walk. I had terrible stomach ache for days, which no medication could take away. My urine was always turning red like blood.

In fact, before this time, when I would go to church I was not willing to praise God with all my heart; I always felt He needed to give me a child before I could worship him fully. The two doctors who attended to me, after the third day of my hospitalization, brought in equipment for surgery. I managed to ask one of them, what would they be looking for during the surgery. He told me *"well since we can not find what is wrong with you, when we tear you open we may be able to detect it."* This statement very much frightened me.

I was very depressed to hear what the doctors had said. I remembered how I then used to reluctantly worship God; now I was between life and death. The Pastor of my church then came to visit me and to pray with me. After they had left, I turned my face to the wall and made a vow, "O Lord my God if you can deliver me from this pain and unknown sickness, I will serve you all the days of my life."

That same day, my condition improved and I was discharged from the hospital. From then on nobody needs to tell me to open my mouth to praise God before I do so at every occasion where God's name is being praised. I thank my God for giving me the grace to keep my vow to this day. God has given me lots of opportunity to minister to women especially, men and children to help me to fulfill my vow.

However, my husband made a bigger vow. After, trying for a long time and all medical treatments seem to have failed, I now decided to go into fasting and praying in sincerity. One early morning on May 1992, my husband advised me seriously to go back to the doctor for another test tube baby (IVF) I did not argue with him. Instead I ran into the room, called a sister who agreed with me in prayer for God to change my husband's mind about me going to the doctor.

At this juncture, I decided to fully depend on God; since all efforts by the doctors had failed. My husband called and booked an appointment. I did not want to disobey but quietly tried to convince him that God will do it. My husband is knowledgeable in the medical area; he then spoke with an angry voice, "Okay, don't go to the doctor, if God will do it without your going to the doctor, I will write a book." Thus, this volume you hold in your hand right now, is in fulfillment of that vow!

I pray this book will touch lives and the anointing will flow in order to break the yoke of everyone reading this book, in Jesus Name. Amen. I agreed with the vow, because, God is performing more miracles now in our generation than he did during the time the Bible was written. Praise be to God forever and ever, Amen. Your miracle is on the way in Jesus name, do not give up please. I then went straight into the room with my hopeless situation; knelt down and said, *"Lord that is a challenge for you..."*

Glory be to God, it was the same month miraculously I got pregnant. I thank God for His faithfulness. However, vows must be accomplished with thanksgiving. After Hannah made the vow she went home and cried no more. Apparently, she had more solid faith in God and believed God had answered her prayers, which really happened. After a vow, one must have concrete faith because God answers prayers.

Thanksgiving:

The Bible says in Ephesians 5:20, *"For in everything give thanks."* And also in 1 Thessalonians 5:18, *"In every thing give thanks: for this is the will of God in Christ Jesus concerning you."* God loves us so much when we give Him thanks, no matter the situation that we are in. God is a good God, He will never give us more than we can handle. He inhabits the praises of his people (Psalm 22:3). During trial and tribulations, giving thanks to God and praising Him in difficult times make the hands of God to move fast on our behalf.

A case in point, is when Paul and Silas were in prison, they rejoiced and sang songs of praise. The Lord came in a different way least expected by anyone to set them free. There is great power in praising God Almighty. There is victory when you praise God in bad situation. I immediately changed my attitude of murmuring and sadness to that of praise and thanking God.

At this time in my life whenever I went to the store, I purposely would go past the area where baby things were displayed and start thanking God that very soon I would also be buying those things. And, of course in this condition my body changed and just in a few months. God blessed me. When the going got tough, I danced for hours praising God and glorifying His ever-living name. He says His grace is sufficient for us.

In the Holy Bible, King Jehoshaphat in 2 Chronicles 20, when great multitude came against him and the people of Israel, proclaimed a fast to pray and seek God's face. God told them to appoint singers and praise Him. As they began to sing and praise him, the Lord set ambushments against their enemies (v. 22) and they were completely destroyed. David knew how to praise God so much that God made his only begotten son Jesus Christ, his descendant. Praising God brings His attention to your needs and problems quickly. He always comes through to defeat the enemies and give you the victory.

I pray today that as you read this book, you will lift up your Holy hands (1 Timothy 2:8) and praise the King of Kings. No matter the situation, God will come through for you today. I will not forget to mention that some of us have anointing for murmuring. God in His mercy does not like those that murmur. (1 Corinthians 10:10). The more one murmurs the more the condition worsens. This is because murmuring has nothing good in store but frustration and depression. It opens a door to lack and destruction.

Giving thanks for what you have not received keeps you focused and strengthens your faith. It encourages and keep your hope going. It keeps your mind at rest and challenges God to prove Himself in your life. I always use the following

In Search of a Child

illustration when sometimes I minister on praises and giving thanks. Before my son was born, I had my brother-in-law's daughter living with me. She was just 18 months old when she came to us.

One day, she asked me for candy as I was driving, I refused. She cried and cried and I told her she could cry all she wanted but that I was not going to give it to her because I did not want to go to the dentist. After about ten minutes of crying, she stopped and started hugging me saying "mama, I love you, you are a good mother." My heart jumped for joy and I decided to quickly give her as many candies, as she required at that time. She caught my heart because of her praises and I then did not mind going to the dentist.

Thanksgiving Day:

I thank the good Lord for everything. I thank God for Americans who set out the last Thursday of every November, to give thanks to God. It is always a big day as it is declared a national Holiday for everyone. In 1986, I decided not to celebrate it. I told my husband that God has not done anything for me to be thankful for. So, there were no plans made.

Fortunately, three days before the Thanksgiving Day, I sat in front of the TV. I accidentally turned on a Christian channel called *700 Club*. I decided to just waste some little time to see what they were showing. I then saw a man, with no legs, I mean from his thighs down was nothing! According to the story, he has just finished a 25 mile marathon. He was raising up his hands hopping real fast to praise the good Lord. Oh, goose bumps came down my body. Right there I was convicted that if a man who has no legs and thighs can praise God, what about me? Dear reader, he lost his legs during the war.

Let us always remember, the good things God has done for us right from when we were born, then we will have lots of reasons to praise His name. Since we have a God that can not fail, praising Him and thanking him for everything can make the impossible to become possible. Thankfulness is the surest way to keeping the flow of blessings in our own life and endeavors. Thankfulness opens the door for the abundance of blessings to flow unto you. Everyday of our lives we should give God thanks, even for waking up in the morning. It is the secret to having the joy of the Lord and to experiencing increased blessing in life.

Let us pray: *I pray to thee O lord, that anyone reading this book at this time, no matter the circumstance should be able to praise you, so that they can receive your abundant blessings in*

Jesus Name. Remember, when praises go up, Blessings comes down!

Emmanuel's Story

I was born and raised in a Christian family, where the only gifts from most family members especially from my mother's side of the family were prayers and going to church. During the years of my up bringing, I learnt something very important from my mother - "Patience." That was the gift of God that enabled me to endure the trials my wife has been narrating.

I met my wife very early in my life; we were in our teens. It was love at first sight. I found out, later that she attended the same elementary school and her grandparents and mine were long time family friends since their youth.

We got married after nine years of courtship. The next fourteen years was a time of test and trial of our faith in God. It was not easy, but I thank my God for giving me the grace, strength and power to stand the test of childlessness. I would like to warn couples, that infertility is not two months or six months after marriage but honestly trying for at least one year before you consider yourself infertile. I know that most research indicates that we are in the age, especially for we Nigerians, where a woman is expected to be pregnant before marriage or right after marriage or else the marriage will be in trouble. This should not be so.

Fourteen years of marriage with no child was not a joke. Being the first son of my family, it was a big stigma. All my younger brothers and sisters had children. The pressure became more than I could endure; but God's Grace was sufficient for me. Our Lord has promised us that our temptations will not be more than we can handle. And that there will always be a means of escape. Choosing my own escape route without waiting for the Lord would have meant losing the woman that I loved so dearly. So, I constantly pleaded with my family for their understanding, patience and prayers.

God Almighty continued to send people our way who encouraged us and prayed with us. To God be the glory, the prayer support increased our faith in the Lord and in February 1993, God Almighty performed the miracle and did what only He can do. We were blessed miraculously when our son Joshua was born and the impossible became possible through the power of God Almighty.

During this entire ordeal, I made a vow on several occasions, that if God should do it I will surely write a book. I thank God for giving my wife and me the grace and power to put this book together and fulfill our vow. We pray it will be a great source of blessings to everyone in Jesus Name.

8
Jesus The Anchor

In several places in the Holy Bible, our Lord Jesus Christ enjoined His disciples and the people to be of good cheer which also means to be of good courage. Each time, they were in a very bad situation. He never told them to be of good cheer when the going was good. The Lord Jesus encouraged everyone all throughout His ministry. As the lover of our souls, He always wants us to be stable in His care. He said, we should cast all our burdens upon him, because he cares for us. Jesus is truly a burden lifter. His name is power. The Bible says:

> **"Wherefore God also hath highly exalted him, and given him a name which is above every name: That at the name of Jesus every knee should bow, of things in heaven, and things in earth, and things under the earth; And that every tongue should confess that Jesus Christ is Lord, to the glory of God the Father" (Philippians 2:9-11).**

There is wonderful power in the name and blood of Jesus Christ. We Christians should not underestimate it. I remember in time of pain and trouble, when I called on the name of Jesus out of sincerity, it worked fast. One such instance, I was in a store one day, all of a sudden, I had severe stomach pain and I wanted to use the restroom real bad. I knew in my heart that I couldn't make it there because of the pain. I then decided to use the great power by calling the name of Jesus. I did three times and instantly God healed me.

Jesus is our anchor. Anchor according to the dictionary means, "something used to provide stability or security." Every knee bows at the mention of the name Jesus. It calms all fears, that every demons of hell dread the name of Jesus. We have the authority as a redeemed child of God to use the name and get tremendous positive results.

Be of Good Cheer:

Proverbs 15:1 says, *"a merry heart makes a cheerful countenance: but by sorrow of the heart the spirit is broken."* God likes us to always have a merry heart. No condition is permanent. He said in Psalm 46:10, that we should be still and know that He is God.

In The Midst Of Great Storm:

Jesus to everyone in Matthew 14:24, 26, 27, *"But the ship was now in the midst of the sea, tossed with waves: for the wind was contrary,"* v. 26, *"And when the disciples saw him walking on the sea, they were troubled, saying, It is a Spirit; and they cried out for fear. But straightway, Jesus spake unto them, saying. Be of good cheer; it is I; be not afraid."* What a wonderful Anchor of our lives!

When Troubled:

2 Corinthians 4:8-9 says, *"We are troubled on every side,, yet not distressed; we are perplexed, but not in despair;..."* Cheerfulness also means joyfulness. Even after our Lord has ascended into heaven, He appeared to Paul in the night when they were in trouble on their way to Rome because their ship was sinking which would have definitely killed everyone. Jesus appeared to Paul in the dream and told him to be of good cheer, that he shall surely testify of him in Jerusalem. Paul took this to heart and used it to also encourage all in the ship according to Acts 27:25.

To The Sick:

Our Lord Jesus said, in Matthew 9:2, *"And, behold they brought to him a man sick of the palsy, lying on a bed: and Jesus seeing their faith said unto the sick of the palsy; Son, BE OF GOOD CHEER thy sins be forgiven thee."* To all of us Jesus said, *"Who his own self bare our sins in his own body on the tree, that we, being dead to sins, should live unto righteousness: by whose stripes ye were healed"* (1 Peter 2:24).

In This World Of Tribulations:

Our Lord Jesus encouraged us to be of good cheer; because He has overcome the world (John 16:33). As I am writing this chapter an old song just came to my heart, which is titled: "I have Anchored My Soul In The Haven Of Rest," by H. L. Gilmour and Geo D. Moore.

> *My soul in sad exile was out on life's sea,*
> *So burdened with sin and distress*
> *Till I heard a sweet voice saying*
> *Make me your choice*
> *And I entered the "Haven of Rest!*

Christy Ogbeide

Chorus:

I've anchored my soul in the "Haven of Rest,"

I'll sail the wide seas no more;

The temp-est may sweep o'er the wild, storm-y deep,

In Je-sus I'm safe ever-er-more. Amen

Verse 2

Oh, come to the Sav-ior, he patiently waits

To save by His power divine

Come, an-chor your soul in the "Ha-ven of rest,"

And say, "My Be-lo-ved is mine." (Chorus)

Verse 3

The song of my soul, since the Lord made me whole,

Has been the old story so blest

Of Je-sus who'll save who-so-ev-er will have

A home in the "Ha-ven of Rest!" (Chorus)

Our great anchor is Jesus Christ. He will never fail you when you whole heartedly trust in Him. The Bible says in Isaiah 43:2,

> **When thou passest through the waters, I will be with thee; and through the rivers, they shall not overflow thee: when thou walkest through**

the fire, thou shalt not be burned; neither shall the flame kindle upon thee."

Like always, the anchor of our soul is ever ready to deliver us. His name is high above every sickness, affliction, oppression from the devil, torment by the devil, diseases, barrenness, cancer, headache, worry, depression to mention but few. Our destiny lies in the arms of God.

The devil and all his demons and cohorts may try to delay our blessings but solid trust on the great anchor can change things around in a second. God Almighty is greater than the Devil. The devil is a creature and God is the creator, a creature can not be greater than his creator. Turn your eyes upon Jesus.

Song:
Turn your eyes upon Jesus, Look full into
His wonderful face,
And the things of this earth shall grow strangely dim,
In the light of His glory and grace.

As you lift up your eyes upon Jesus and turn to His precious love and sacrifice on the tree of Calvary, you have no excuse but to embrace his tender love and promises. I pray that the blood of Jesus that was shed will not be in vain in our lives in Jesus' Name. Amen. His divine power will continue to aid you in everything you do. At this juncture, pause and pray this prayer:

> *Lord, I submit to your higher power and authority in Jesus Name. So that I may be above reach for Satan and his cohorts in Jesus Name. Amen.*

Prayer solidifies your anchor on Jesus. Every one should constantly and continuously, pray without ceasing. At the later part of my trial, when I had tried everything humanly possible, I then learnt to trust in Jesus, the miracle worker. Don't use man or woman as your anchor, especially running from one pastor to another for a miracle to happen, only believe, all things are possible. Focus on Jesus He will never let you down.

Fake Preachers:

It is dangerous to focus on preachers, pastors, and so on. In the last days, the Bible says, many shall come in my name; the Bible warns us that some are agents of the devil. I remember traveling from one city to another to meet a so-called man of God who was reputed to be a miracle-worker, it was a bad

In Search of a Child

experience. He asked for so much money, took about thirty of us in number (mostly women), at midnight to a beach to roll on the sand, in order to receive our miracles. After all that my condition grew worse.

Another case in point, was when I traveled to meet another so-called man of God, he also took a lot of money for the prayers he was going to offer for me to get my miracle. At about 9:00 PM he took me to a burial ground to pray for me. Actually, it is only now that I know better that I realize it was all rituals.

Then funny enough I heard strange voices telling me I will surely have a child. This was in 1990 in my country, Nigeria. Oh, it is unbelievable that many fake preachers also brought other people to the burial ground for prayers so to say. The place was crowded like a grocery store. I thought then, "Yes this must be it! After all this my problem will be over." Little did I know that I was adding more problems to myself. Thank you Lord for delivering me. The only way out is total surrender to the Lord. Do not be deceived, only Jesus can save. He only has the answer. Seek him first, all other things will be added unto you.

As I traveled back to the United States, I had a dream that the same pastor was stealing from my purse. I woke up ashamed of myself after spending thousands of dollars traveling to meet him. These fake preachers will promise Heaven and earth but can not deliver. The Bible tells us that we should discern the spirit if it is of God or not. They are many out there, deceiving people and unknown to their victims initiating them into occultism of all sorts, in the name of giving solutions to their problems.

They are few men of God out there who can really agree with you in sincere prayers to our never-failing God, who answers prayers, then the anointing will destroy every yoke in your life. Such true laborers of God are very few. God is still using them to glorify His name. He said, in His Word that we should not despise His prophets (2 Chronicles 20:20).

Jesus the Anchor is the great Deliverer. When you turn all to Him, He will cleanse you and bless you. After you have received your miracle, remember to share it. Some He would heal and ask them to go and tell no one. He knows when to give them the command to tell people. Devil is wicked and can contest your blessing.

One day I had a dream. In the dream, my womb was shown to me, and the voice said, "you will have a baby but do not tell anybody. I woke up very happy and decided to tell just one of our Pastor family friends. Oh, that month I bled like never before. It took seven years before the dream came to materialize in the physical. God is very faithful; He does not like disobedience. Using Jesus His only begotten son as your anchor, His will in your life will surely be accomplished. He did not only make miracles to happen in your life but also gives you eternal life.

Hell is real, Heaven is real. Hell or Heaven is just a heartbeat away. God has given everyone a choice. I pray your own choice, no matter the circumstance would be to follow Jesus to the end. The Holy Bible says, He (she) that endures to the end will be saved and will also gain the crown of life.

When the last breath is taken, there is no repentance in the grave. So, as you read this book, if you know in your heart that you have not received Jesus Christ as your Lord and personal Savior and you have not invited Him to come into your life, please do so today.

Read John 3:16 and Romans 10:9-10. Mean it and pray it with all your heart. Please do so today. Our heavenly father is faithful, He will forgive you all your sins. 1 John 1:9 says it all.

Please do so today; tomorrow may be too late. Forget about your past, learn from your past mistakes because where you are going is more important. Run to a living Church, tell the Holy

Spirit to direct you and publicly come out to declare the name of Jesus Christ.

Say this prayer and mean it from your heart:

> *Lord Jesus I come to you just as I am. I am very sorry for my sins. I repent from them all. With my mouth I confess that Jesus you are Lord; in my heart I believe that God raised you from the dead and I am saved. Thank you Jesus for saving me. Come and take control of my life and bless me, in Jesus Name. Amen.*

I pray that the blood of Jesus will overtake your subconsciousness and consciousness, so you can give your heartand your soul to He who is able to keep you from failing.

> **"Now unto him that is able to keep you from falling, and to present you faultless before the presence of his glory with exceeding joy, To the only wise God our Savior, be glory and majesty, dominion and power, both now and ever. Amen" (Jude 24-25).**

9
God Knows My Telephone Number

On March 6, 1987, unable to face the extremities of life, I concluded that life was not worth living. To some degree we have all leaned towards this direction at one time or the other in our life. I then contemplated ending my life, or just to run away as far as I could from the problem I was facing. I very much believed that my childlessness had brought me too much shame and reproach that I could not bear it any more. I looked up to heaven and it did not seem that any answer was coming as fast as I wanted.

At this time of my life, it seemed that I could not go on, that I just could not take it anymore. My coping skill was failing me very fast. It happens always - the pain of terminal diseases, the pain of childlessness, the pain of a broken marriage etc.; all can be very painful, but surely we need God's wisdom to direct us at this juncture. James 1:5 says, *"But if any of you lack wisdom, let him ask of God, who gives to all men generously and without reproach, and it will be given to him."*

Sometimes these pains are so severe that we really need God's grace and strength to deal with them. We even have difficulty accepting these pains, let alone understanding them. We need at this time; insights into God's wisdom in order for us to keep living.

Wisdom

Wisdom means something much more than knowledge or intellectual ability, which is often found to be totally inadequate in dealing with life's deepest problems. At this stage of my life, I was full of constant doubts and fear. I was battered and bruised by the pressures and difficulties of life. My problem was overwhelming me and I had lots of questions but no immediate answer, not even the best doctors could help me; from my heart I always asked God, "Why Lord, why me? Why this, why now? Why on earth is this happening to me? Am I the worst sinner on earth? See! The other women are getting pregnant so fast that they do not even want to have children anymore. Are they better than me? Am I not also your daughter?"

I came to God with these questions and many more. I came looking for answers, for wisdom to understand, for power and strength to carry on and accept my condition. Many feel that it is out of place to ask God questions. It is not scriptural that we

In Search of a Child

shouldn't, only that we can not question God's authority because He is in-charge and does whatever pleases Him.

Certainly, questions are normal, but we must not stay there. We must never second-guess God in anything. Many times when you ask Him, He always will come to speak with you through revelations, to give you answers. In my case, I asked and he kept telling me, "I am with you."

One day, I said, "O Lord, if you are really with me, let me get pregnant today." We should know that God's time is the best in everything.

Doubting:

Doubting according to the dictionary means our inner uncertainty about an issue. When we doubt we are uncertain whether we really want the answer God has for us or not. Doubting can lead to fear and fear really weakens faith. You need much faith at this time. The word doubting means *"to be divided, to be at variance with yourself."* When things are going well doubters put God on the shelf, but in crisis, they turn to God. We must have faith and not doubt; especially if our miracle seems delayed or not instantly answered.

Salvation:

On November 1986, after much preaching from a pastor friend, I decided to completely give my life to Christ. Giving your life to Christ automatically enlists you in God's army that must be in the forefront of the battle to fight against Satan and his demonic slaves until Jesus comes. On the other hand, the devil is enlisting people that will inherit hell fire with him through lies and deceit. We Christians should be very happy because the captain of our army is Jesus and has defeated Satan two thousand years ago. John 10:10 says, *"The thief cometh not, but for to steal, and to kill and to destroy: I am come that they might have life, and that they might have it more abundantly."*

The day I came out in my church to openly declare for Jesus, I was very happy. I said, "Yes, all troubles are gone." I underestimated the fact that Satan will now wage war against me all the more. Just five months later, I got tired of life and there was a voice that kept telling me Jesus was not real and that taking my life was an easy escape from my problems. I yielded to the voice.

Please reader, and all true men of God, take your new converts seriously. Do a constant follow-up; do not leave them alone. Spend time with them and make sure for, at least, one whole year that they are soaked in the Word of God. In so doing, it will be easy for them not to hear any other voice but that of God.

Suicide:

Taking one's life is an automatic entrance to hell. We did not create ourselves and do not have the right to take our lives. We are peculiar people made in the image of God, so we resemble Him.

On this particular day, I was tired of life completely. After my University degree, I decided to go and study cosCetology. On March 6, 1987, which was a Saturday, I decided to really be nice to all my friends at the school because this was going to be the last day they would see me. I thought of the quickest way to end my life and decided to go to the store to get some medicine that will act quickly and kill me almost immediately.

At 5:00 PM that evening, I decided to wear my best nightgown, one that I would like to die in. I locked all the doors and window.

Surprisingly, my husband was scheduled to work till 2:00 AM that morning contrary to his usual former closing hours of 11:00 PM. I automatically became sick, because a sick mind is a sick body. I could feel my temperature was rising and I desperately wanted to end my life. I placed the medicine with a cup of water by my bedside and decided to take it immediately.

At 7:00 PM I took up the cup of water and the medicine, then I heard a voice, *"Don't do that, you remember that your grandmother loves you."* I decided to live for just one more hour. I lay down on the bed with all lights off just by myself.

At 8:00 PM approximately, I said, "This is it, I must take my life now." A voice spoke, *"Don't you remember your husband loves you."* Oh, I then started thinking of how patient my husband has been, very caring and loving. He is really a special God-sent husband to me. I then decided to live one more hour.

At exactly 9:00 PM - I knew the time because a clock was in front of me - my phone rang. Someone on the other end said, "Can I speak to Christy and Christy alone." In a rude tone I answered, "Yes," This is because whoever the person was, was delaying my plan to end my life. The person also repeated my phone number to me for confirmation. He then said, *"I am asked to call this number now."*

The following was the dialogue that took place that evening. God knows this is nothing but the truth. To God be all the glory and honor forever and ever Amen.

Unknown Person: Can I pray with you?

Me: Well, if you want, you can pray.

In Search of a Child

He prayed and prayed and prayed and never wanted to stop praying. I then heard a voice in my inner self, "This person has been praying for you, could you pay attention to him and listen attentively." I then decided to move myself and take the telephone to the living room from the bedroom.

In the living room, I sat down angry but quiet, because this unknown person would not stop praying. When he finished, it had been over an hour and a half since he had been praying. I was annoyed because he was truly delaying me from taking my life. Then I asked him in a rude voice:

Me: Who are you? Are you a white man? If you are a white man you should know that it is too late to call any one in America? (This is because in America, unless you are really familiar with the person and they are expecting your call, it is just too late to call anyone after 9:00 PM.)

Unknown Person: (No answer, but a question) Do you pay your tithes?

Me: Well, I don't think I have time for that, I do not even have money to pay all my bills talk less of paying tithes. Please, leave me alone.

Unknown Person: Well, there is a curse for those that do not pay tithes. It is also a commandment that comes with blessings.

Me: Well, I just told you that I don't have money, talk less of paying tithes.

Unknown Person: It is good to pay your tithes. Let me pray with you for God to forgive you for not paying your tithes. And he prayed.

At this time, I looked at the wall clock in front of me it was 11:45 PM.

Unknown Person: There is something in your mouth that you want to say.

Me: Well, there is nothing in my mouth, and I just told you that I do not have money to donate or contribute to you. (Thinking that he was asking me for money.)

Unknown Person: (No answer) I want you to close your eyes and you will see something and then say it out.

Me: I then closed my eyes and saw some letters that were not written in English language but I was able to read them.

Then all of a sudden the person on the other end said: *Yes that is it.*

At this juncture, I will add here that I had never spoken in tongues before in my life neither did I believe in it. I was never interested.

Coming from an Anglican (Episcopal) and Baptist background, I did not believe in speaking in tongues. It was not

In Search of a Child

in our doctrine. We always laughed at those who claimedd to be speaking in tongues.

Oh, now I know the gift of speaking in tongues is real. Do not joke about it or with it. It will grieve the Holy Spirit. Read Mark 16:17, *"And these signs shall follow them that believe; In my name shall they cast out devils; they shall speak with new tongues."*

Acts 2:4, *"And they were all filled with the Holy Ghost and began to speak with other tongues, as the Spirit gave them utterance."*

Acts 10:45, *"And they of the circumcision which believed were astonished, as many as came with Peter, because that on the Gentiles also was poured out the gift of the Holy Ghost."*

This is a gift that everyone who does not understand what it means should go to God and ask Him. The blessed Holy Spirit will reveal the true divine knowledge and wisdom, and will bring to your understanding the importance of speaking in tongues. It doesn't mean if you do not speak in tongues you will not enter into heaven but ask the Holy Spirit any thing you do not understand He will teach you all things (John 14:26).

Me: I immediately felt great warmth all over my body, as I spoke those words out of my mouth.

At that instant I heard a voice saying, "It is not real, this is all fake." May we never hear the voice of the devil in Jesus Name. Immediately that thought came to my heart, the warmth over my body then turned to hot sweat and was burning like fire. My whole body was burning.

Dear reader, it was not funny, it was really hot. Each drop of sweat flowing down from my face was like fire. I kept shouting, my body is burning, my body is burning. I then quickly pulled off my nightgown that I was wearing, which I wanted to die in. I instantly started shouting, asking, "Am I still in my apartment?"

Unknown Person: Yes you are!

The fire was still burning in my body. What an experience. The phone was going off and on, I was shouting real badly. My whole body was hot. Oh! It was real. Holy Ghost is power. I was truly baptized with Holy Ghost fire that day. Never you underestimate the power of God. It is real. I then passed out.

I finally woke up in the bathroom about 25ft from where I was sitting. All alone, the phone went dead. I did not understand where I was. When I finally got up, I picked up the phone which was on one end of the bathroom, shakily, I said, "Hello!"

Unknown Person: Yes, I am still here!

In Search of a Child

Turning my eyes drowsily up to the wall clock, it was 1:20 AM in the morning. I became very afraid of this unknown person, and a question went through my mind that who sent him. Not knowing who has been speaking to me for the past hours. Very much afraid and shaking, and becoming more polite, I proceeded:

Me: Sir, who are you?

Unknown Person: (Ignored my question) I want you Christy, to pray for me so I can continue to reach other people for God.

Me: No, sir, you pray for me, because this is a new thing that just happened to me.

Unknown Person: You, pray for me, because God is going to use you mightily to win more souls for Him.

Me: I prayed for him, not knowing even what I was saying. After praying, I said could I know your name and phone number sir, so that I can be calling you for prayers? Do you go to church? Who are you really? Can I know you better? Are you a member of my Church? Will you be in Church tomorrow?

Unknown Person: Well, I am always the first to be in the Church. As for you knowing me? You have already known me in the Lord.

Then he hanged up the phone. I looked at the wall clock it was 2:30 AM Oh! I held on to the phone for a long time;

frightened, because I did not understand what had just happened to me. Who had been talking with me? I questioned?

Anyway, the first thing that came to my mind was to go and take that suicide medication and flush it down the toilet, which I did immediately. I then called my pastor friend to reveal the whole ordeal of about five hours. Oh, God bless his heart. It was about 2:30 AM when I called him. He was very happy and gave me scriptures and admonished me. He rejoiced with me and prayed for me. Then I started speaking in the heavenly language as the Holy Ghost gave me utterance.

It was about 3.00 AM when my precious husband got back from work. He opened the door and wondered why I was not asleep. I told him a little bit of my encounter the past few hours and instead of laughing at me like I thought he would, he was rejoicing with me.

My husband like me never believed in speaking in tongues. He then told me that as he was coming from work, he heard a voice that said that he should pray for me. And he truly prayed while driving the 35 miles on his way home. That prayer really worked.

We prayed together that night and thanked God for sparing my life and for the encounter, which only He knows about.

In Search of a Child

Exactly, three months later, at about 7.00 AM in the morning, the unknown person called again, *"Can, I pray with Christy and Christy alone?"* Quickly I said, "Yes." And he prayed and prayed and hung up the phone. I said in my heart, "God, who is this?" I then thanked God for everything.

One day, a friend gave me a book; it was also a story of a woman who wanted to commit suicide because of the trials she was going through. Right then, the lord gave her a phone number and a name, that she must call. She never knew whose number it was. She reluctantly obeyed and called. She told God, if there was no answer, she will have to do what she wanted to do.

As the phone rang it was a pay phone; a minister of God was walking into a restaurant. He quickly ran to the pay phone just to tell the person on the other end that it was a pay phone and nobody is there to answer the call.

As he picked the phone and said hello, the woman at the other end asked, *"Can I speak to so and so, mentioning the real name of the minister."* The minister was astonished while acknowledging he was the one. He then asked, "What is the matter and who are you. How did you know I was coming to this restaurant? The woman answered, "Well the Lord gave me this name and number to call and that the person must come to my house immediately or....," she would end her life. The minister ran as fast as he could to the woman's house.

Praise God, she surrendered her life to Jesus. Right now, she is on fire for the Lord. God Almighty knows all you are going through. He truly knows your name, address and phone number. He has promised that, *"Behold, I have engraved thee upon the palms of my hands; thy walls (problems) are continually before me"* (Isaiah 49:16).

At the times of trials, we should stand on the Word of God and claim all his promises especially concerning our problems. God is never slack in keeping His promise. He is the El-shaddai, the Mighty One and the ever-living Father. He said we should remind Him of his words to perform.

Isaiah 43:26 declares, *"Put me in remembrance: let us plead together: declare thou; that thou mayest be justified."* If you remind God of what He promised you, He will do it. Faith without works is dead. The work really is to believe and stand on His promises.

My grandmother at 92 years old, stood on the promises of God, and declared that she would not die until she saw my child. Such faith! She challenged God! There was a time she passed away but later woke up again. When I traveled to Nigeria, I asked her, "Mama, how come you woke up. I thought they said you passed away." She answered me and said, "Yes." But that as she was going through a narrow path like a tunnel, she saw a man who told her to go back that it was not yet time. That was in 1991. I knew then that I would surely have children from God.

The hard work of praying fervently without ceasing and giving up surely came to pass. She prayed and prayed. Don't give up please, no matter the situation, it pays to be persistent. Luke 18:1 says, *"Men ought always to pray and not to faint."*

I am blessed that my grandmother, Princess Omoruwa Agho Ayanru finally passed away on February 26, 1997 at the age of 110, after seeing and carrying my child Joshua Ogbeide, on three separate occasions when we went to Nigeria.

Just like Simon in the Bible, the first time she saw my child she said, "Now I can depart from this world." Through prayers and waiting faithfully, she saw my promised child.

The Lord said in Jeremiah 1:12, that he will quicken his word to perform in our lives. Stand on the promises of God, believe in His word and it shall come to pass. I like the verses in the Bible that say, *"and it came to pass."* It will only come to pass when there is persistence in prayers and trust in the never failing God, who very much desire that none of His children should perish but all come to repentance and have His saving grace. There are many fulfillment in the Word of God.

Tongue:

There is power in the tongue. Mind what you say and prophesy to yourself. The Bible says *"life and death is in the power of the tongue"* that we will get what we say. If you keep saying, "I know I must have children." Believe it, and it shall surely come to pass.

Our Lord God and Father of all, told us in the Bible that whatsoever we ask or desire we shall receive. Please, speak to every mountain to move, in Jesus name. Surely it shall move. Knowing what I know now, I thank my God.

Looking back now, seeing where the good Lord has brought me from, I am very grateful for each moment. I would have been dead and forgotten by now. But our Lord saw me through. He will surely see you through. He is no respecter of persons, but as many as turn to Him, he shall no wise cast out. The Stone that the builders rejected has now become the Head Cornerstone. Glory and honor be unto our Lord forever and ever Amen.

My Miracle Boy Joshua

Born February 12, 1993, is really a blessing and a great and wonderful miracle from our Lord. Anointed of God and divinely is growing in wisdom and stature and favor with God and man. I thank the Lord, because "IT CAME TO PASS."

Letter:

A letter came from my doctor August 15, 1994 in which he included a new IVF program for me. I later wrote back with a picture of my son. He reply to me was as follows:

Re: Christy Ogbeide
***Clinic No. 1505241

Dear Christy:

Thank you for your letter in January. It is good to know that you finally conceived and have a child. I am very happy that this has happened and I feel that you have certainly been blessed. Thanks again for letting us know of your good fortune:

Sincerely:
Signed
Dr. Whitesides

Dr. Whitesides was a very good doctor, who initially confirmed that I could not have a normal pregnancy, but when Dr. Jesus Christ came and took over my case, miracle happened. I thank God for everything and even for the life of the doctor.

10

Prayer and Fasting - "The Key to the Impossible"

Prayer is communicating with God. If we do not pray we can not get any answer from God. Prayer and fasting make the impossible to become possible. In a relationship where there is no communication it always ends up in disaster. Talking with our heavenly father always and every time should solidify our relationship with Him. When we breathe we should breathe prayers. You can also pray together as a family. As the saying goes, "a family that prays together, stays together."

Why Do We Pray?

The purpose of prayer is to get God's will to be done in our lives, to draw God's attention to our needs and lives. It is pleasing to God when we pray. It is an act of worship, not just an expression of our wants and needs. We pray to get direction and wisdom from God.

We pray to turn situations around, Isaiah 38:2, *"Then Hezekiah turned his face toward the wall, and prayed unto the*

Lord." We pray for open doors; we pray to conquer Satan, when in distress and confused and when in trouble pray. (Jeremiah 33:3) We pray in times of war to get victory. There are countless reasons why we must pray. In terms of crisis, trials and tribulations we need more time to pray or we become prey to those circumstances.

Our Lord Jesus taught the disciples how to pray. Matthew 6:9-13, *"After this manner therefore pray ye: Our father which art in heaven, Hallowed be thy name..."* We should give adoration and praises to God as we start to pray. Acknowledge Him as King of Kings and creator of heaven and earth. We then confess our sins and ask God to forgive us as we forgive others. We must then ask God for His divine protection and guidance each day.

Where To Pray:

We can pray everywhere; as God's children, God is always with us. 1 Tim. 2:8, says, *"I will therefore that men pray every where..."* We can pray in the closet (Matthew 6:6); In the temple - Church/Fellowship - (Luke 18:10, Psalm 26:12).

When To We Pray:

Always:

Luke 18:1 and 1 Thessalonians 5:17 say we should pray without ceasing. We should pray in the mornings (Psalm 5:3); At noon and in the evening (Psalm 55:17). Pray daily - Psalm 86:3 says, *"Be merciful unto me, O Lord: for I cry unto thee daily."* We should pray Day and Night - Psalm 88:1-3, Finally, we should pray In and Out of Season, at least three times a day, Daniel 6:10, *"...He kneeled upon his knees three times a day, and prayed, and gave thanks before his God, as he did aforetime."*

Attitude In Prayer

There are many prayer postures in the Bible. We can pray standing with outstretched hands (1 Kings 8:22); Kneeling (Dan. 6:10); Standing (Luke 18:11); Sitting (2 Sam 7:18); Bowing the Head (Genesis 24:26); We can pray Lifting The eyes to Heaven John 17:1 says, *These words spake Jesus, and lifted up his eyes to heaven and said, Father, the hour is come; glorify thy Son, that thy Son also may glorify thee."* We can pray falling on the Ground, Genesis 17:3, *"And Abram fell on his face: and God talked with him saying..."*

The important thing is not the posture of the body but the posture of your heart. As you start to pray, remember that you are talking to a sovereign God, so respect and honor His presence. As Christians there shouldn't be any excuse not to find time to pray. Praying is like putting money in the bank.

There is no prayer that God does not hear, Isaiah 58:9, *"When you call upon me, I shall answer you."* We are warned however in the book of James not to pray amiss. No Christian should wait until when trouble knocks at the door before praying. Do not depend solely upon the prayers of others to carry you through your trials. Prayer of agreement works, but have confidence to know that God loves and hears you when you pray.

Essentials For Effective Prayer

<u>Pray Without Doubting</u> - This means we must pray in faith; no "disputing" that is no doubting whether God can do it or not. God is able more abundantly to do all things.

<u>Without Wrath</u> - means we must be in good terms with one another (Matthew 18). A person who is constantly having trouble with other believers, who is a troublemaker rather than a peacemaker, can not pray and get answers from God. (Mark 11:24-25).

<u>Confess Your Sins</u> - Psalm 66:18, *"If I regard iniquity in my heart, the Lord will not hear me."* Confessing and forsaking our sins brings quick results (Proverbs 28:13). It is one principle of our Ministry. If we spend more time preparing to pray and getting our hearts right before God, our prayers would be more effective.

Fasting

Fasting is for the purpose of drawing you from the natural into the spiritual. It is to stimulate the spiritual faculties of those who seek after God, and to strengthen and implement prayer. Fasting is necessary because our Lord Jesus said, many demons can not be cast away through prayers alone but through fasting and praying (Mark 9:29). As you fast always remember to thank God for the answer to your request.

Benefits Of Fasting:

"Is not this the fast that I have chosen? to loose the bands of wickedness, to undo the heavy burdens, and to let the oppressed go free, and that ye break every yoke?" (Isaiah 58:6).

It gives God's children spiritual and physical blessings, deliverance from spiritual burdens and strong enough faith to cast out demons. Fasting can be a deciding factor for a very negative situation.

In Acts 27, fasting saved 276 people that could have perished in the sea. Through fasting you can receive healing and undo the bands of the wicked (Isaiah 58:6); It brings assurance of the faith that brings the answer; and makes supernatural things to happen.

There is great power in fasting - it delivers you from the power of Satan and casts out the devil. Mark 9:29, says, *"And he said unto them, this kind can come forth by nothing, but by prayer and fasting."* It will move every mountain that stands on the way of your blessing. It brings about new anointing. A case in point is after Elijah fasted forty days and forty nights, he received a new anointing (1 Kings 19).

Even our Savior Jesus Christ, before going into His full time Ministry (Luke 4:1-13), fasted forty days and forty nights, thereby making the impossible to become possible by winning back what Adam had lost. I hear people say, "We don't have need to fast because Jesus has fasted for us." This is wrong. We have lots of needs to fast. We must follow the example of our Master, Jesus Christ.

Fasting crucifies the flesh and the Spirit of God will rise in you. The Lord Jesus said, "Man does not live by bread alone but by every word that proceeds from the mouth of God" (Luke 4:4). We should be careful as Christians not to neglect this aspect of worshipping God.

It is also wrong for any one to pay others to fast for them like some churches do. Fast for yourself, others can join to make the fasting more powerful. The Bible says, *"iron sharpens iron"* (Proverbs 27:17). Oh! fasting brings great and quick results and turns away the anger of God (Jonah 3:5-10).

Fasting makes God move faster to fight our battles. In 1 Samuel 7:1-13, the children of Israel fasted and prayed and lo, the Lord came on the scene, and thundered a great thunder against the Philistines. The enemy of Israel was put into confusion and they were defeated. They never came against the Israelites from then on. So, God will put all the enemies of our souls, the devil and all his demonic servants into confusion and humiliation in Jesus Name! Amen. Fasting helps to win battles and puts the enemy to flight (Judges 20).

Sanctification

God recognizes you when you fast (Acts 10:9-18). Cornelius fasted, prayed and gave alms and lo, an angel was sent to Peter in a vision to go and minister to him. This episode brought salvation to the Gentiles. All hope seemed to have gone for the Jews in the days of Esther for the King has signed a document in which Haman's men had authority to destroy all who were of that race. But Esther and her maidens with Mordecai her uncle fasted three days and nights and then risking her own life made the petition before the King (Esther 4:16-17).

Not only were her people saved but also the wicked Haman, was hanged on His own gallons that he made for Mordecai and his people. I thank the good Lord for our Ministry. We believe very much in prayers and fasting. We declare fasting as the Lord leads and it has brought tremendous and countless miracles to the glory of God the father Almighty.

During my trials especially when all hope was gone, and the doctor on July 19, 1991, sent me a letter from the hospital after a painful surgery that there was no way for me to have any child naturally, except through IVF program; I resorted to more fasting and praying. That was the only source left.

The major cause of the problem, cyst and scar tissues had rendered my fallopian tubes useless. I thank God that he turned my hopeless and impossible situation to be possible. Scar tissues do not have medications or any means to get them out.

In Search of a Child

Glory be to God, doctor Jesus cleared out my scar tissues with spiritual surgery and the miracle came to be. Dr. Jesus will do the same for you today, believe in God. All is well. When everything else fails, God will continue to prevail.

At this juncture, I will encourage every reader to be in tune with the Lord. Don't fast for fasting sake. Fast with a purpose that you will like to accomplish with the fasting. List your entire prayer request and believe God can do everything at His precious appointed time.

The thoughts God Almighty has for you is of good and not of evil (Jeremiah 29:11). As long as God directs you he will give you the strength to complete the fasting. No prayer is wasted. God honors Christians who take fasting and praying serious. Battles are won on your knees. I pray God, to honor your petitions as you read this book. Amen. Let your tribute to Him be taken from Psalm 121:1-2 which says, "I will lift up mine eyes unto the hills, from whence cometh my help? My help cometh from the Lord, which made heaven and earth."

Fasting and praying has become part of my life. I have received both spiritual and physical blessings. The results that follow fasting are always great. Until today, it seems like I am dreaming. However, during my baby's dedication, I read Psalm 126:1-3 (as the scripture of the day) which says,

> "When the Lord turned again the captivity of Zion We were like them that dream, Then was our mouth filled with laughter, and our tongue with singing: then said they among the heathen, The Lord hath done great things for them. The Lord hath done great things for us; Whereof we are glad."

Actually, there is no conclusion to this testimonial book. This is because we can not say it all in few pages. However, for more information, clarification, speaking engagements, and distribution of this book, please contact:

Dr. and Mrs. Emmanuel Ogbeide

Amazing Testimonies

Dear Sister Christy:

Thank you for sharing your testimony during a convention. It really blessed and encouraged me to keep trusting in the Lord and never to give up.

After listening to your testimony, I went on my knees and asked God to bless me just like He blessed you. Praise God, few months later I got pregnant and now I am a happy mother of a beautiful daughter after five years of barrenness. The good Lord did it for me, glory be to God.
Sister B. M., Nigeria.

Dear beloved Dr. & Mrs. Ogbeide:

Your book, "In Search of a Child" is truly an inspiration of the Holy Spirit the teacher. We join you to thank God and proclaim His faithfulness to those who believe in Him. God is going to use you mightily in all things. Keep growing in both things of God and of man.

Our sincere regards to our miracle brother - Joshua.
Mr. & Mrs. M. Ibe, Houston.

Dear Reader:

In 1995 a friend gave me a video tape that narrated the testimony of how God blessed Sister Christy after 14 years of barrenness. It starred up my faith, and strengthened me the more. To God be the glory few months later I was blessed with triplets. Do not give up, what God did for Sarah, Christy and me, he can do for you in Jesus name. Amen. May the good Lord strengthen you while you wait on Him, in Jesus Name. Amen.

Sister J. A., New Jersey

Appreciation

I thank the Lord, for being in the business of blessing His children. I thank the lord for giving my husband and me the opportunity to write this book about our miracle son. He was truly delighted and a proud father, being our first child; we truly thank the good Lord for putting a new song in our mouth. God is a great promise Keeper, a faithful God indeed forever and ever. Amen

Praise Ye the Lord.
Glory Be To God Forever and Ever! Amen.

"For I am persuaded, that neither death, nor life, nor angels, nor Principalities, nor powers, nor things present, nor things to come nor height, nor depth nor any other creature, shall be able to separate us from the love of God, Which is in Christ Jesus Our Lord."

Romans. 8:38-39

<u>Commitment:</u>

Dear beloved Dr. & Mrs. Ogbeide

Your book, *In Search Of a Child* is truly an inspiration of the Holy Spirit, the teacher. We join you to thank God and proclaim his faithfulness to those who believe in Him. God is going to use you mightily in all things. Keep growing in both things of God and of man.

Our sincere regards to our miracle brother - Joshua

Mr. And Mrs. M. Ibe

About the Author

Christy Ogbeide was called into the ministry in 1991. She is the founder of El-Shaddai Ministry, a prayer and intercessory ministry committed to soul winning, teaching and counseling women. Christy, a woman who loves God, is married and lives with her husband, Dr. Emmanuel Ogbeide and their miracle son, Joshua in Houston, Texas.

She got her BBA in 1984 from Texas Woman's University, Denton, Texas in Business and Economics. In 1997, she got her MA degree in Counseling form Prairie View A&M University, Prairie View, Texas, with honors. She also has various other degrees in Computer and Cosmetology. Presently, she is an Assistant Clinical Supervisor. Christy, who loves to sing, preach, teach and win souls for the Lord, is fully committed to the work, which God has called her to do. She believes that praising God always in songs produces faster response from the Lord.

Printed in the United States
22221LVS00005B/211-222